MASTER THAI ALPHABET

A Handwriting Practice Workbook

Perfect your calligraphy skills in both the traditional and modern Thai writing styles and dive deeper into the language of Thailand

by Lang Workbooks

ISBN: 9781679065699

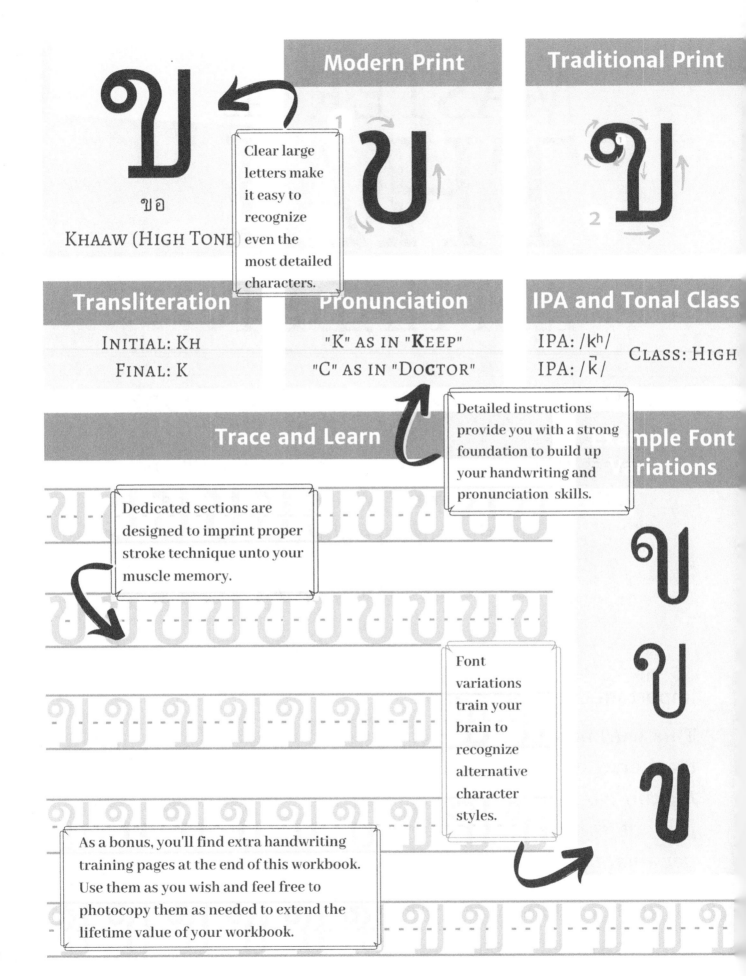

ขอ

KHAAW (HIGH TONE)

Clear large letters make it easy to recognize even the most detailed characters.

Transliteration

INITIAL: KH
FINAL: K

Pronunciation

"K" AS IN "KEEP"
"C" AS IN "DOCTOR"

IPA and Tonal Class

IPA: /kʰ/
IPA: /k̄/

CLASS: HIGH

Detailed instructions provide you with a strong foundation to build up your handwriting and pronunciation skills.

Trace and Learn

mple Font riations

Dedicated sections are designed to imprint proper stroke technique unto your muscle memory.

Font variations train your brain to recognize alternative character styles.

As a bonus, you'll find extra handwriting training pages at the end of this workbook. Use them as you wish and feel free to photocopy them as needed to extend the lifetime value of your workbook.

Workbook Index

· ·

กอ

GAAW (MID TONE)

Modern Print

Traditional Print

Transliteration

INITIAL: K

FINAL: K

Pronunciation

"C" AS IN "**C**AT"

"C" AS IN "DO**C**TOR"

IPA and Tonal Class

IPA: /k/

IPA: /k̄/

CLASS: MID

Trace and Learn

Example Font Variations

ฃ

ขอ

KHAAW (HIGH TONE)

Modern Print

Traditional Print

Transliteration

INITIAL: KH
FINAL: K

Pronunciation

"K" AS IN "KEEP"
"C" AS IN "DOCTOR"

IPA and Tonal Class

IPA: /kʰ/
IPA: /k̄/

CLASS: HIGH

Trace and Learn

ฃ ฃ ฃ ฃ ฃ ฃ ฃ ฃ ฃ ฃ ฃ

ฃ ฃ ฃ ฃ ฃ ฃ ฃ ฃ ฃ ฃ ฃ

ฃ ฃ ฃ ฃ ฃ ฃ ฃ ฃ ฃ ฃ

ฃ ฃ ฃ ฃ ฃ ฃ ฃ ฃ ฃ ฃ

ฃ ฃ ฃ ฃ ฃ ฃ ฃ ฃ ฃ ฃ ฃ ฃ

Example Font Variations

Obsolete Letter	Modern Print	Traditional Print

ฃอ

KHAAW (HIGH TONE)

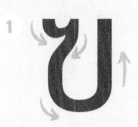

Transliteration	Pronunciation	IPA and Tonal Class
INITIAL: KH FINAL: K	"K" AS IN "**K**EEP" "C" AS IN "DO**C**TOR"	IPA: /kʰ/ IPA: /k̄/ CLASS: HIGH

Trace and Learn

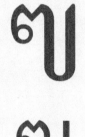

ឋ ឋ ឋ ឋ ឋ ឋ ឋ ឋ ឋ ឋ ឋ ឋ ឋ ឋ ឋ

ឋ

ឋ

ឋ

ឍ ឍ ឍ ឍ ឍ ឍ ឍ ឍ ឍ ឍ ឍ

ឍ

ឍ

ឍ

ឍ

ค

คอ

KHAAW (LOW TONE)

Modern Print

Traditional Print

Transliteration

INITIAL: KH
FINAL: K

Pronunciation

"K" AS IN "KEEP"
"C" AS IN "DOCTOR"

IPA and Tonal Class

IPA: /kʰ/
IPA: /k̄/

CLASS: LOW

Trace and Learn

Example Font Variations

Obsolete Letter	Modern Print	Traditional Print
 ศ อ **KHAAW (LOW TONE)**		

Transliteration	Pronunciation	IPA and Tonal Class
INITIAL: KH FINAL: K	"K" AS IN "**KEEP**" "C" AS IN "DO**C**TOR"	IPA: /kʰ/ IPA: /k̄/ CLASS: LOW

Trace and Learn

ฆอ

KHAAW (LOW TONE)

Transliteration

INITIAL: KH
FINAL: K

Pronunciation

"K" AS IN "KEEP"
"C" AS IN "DOCTOR"

IPA and Tonal Class

IPA: /kʰ/
IPA: /k̄/

CLASS: LOW

Trace and Learn

Example Font Variations

14

ง

งอ

NGAAW (LOW TONE)

Transliteration

INITIAL: NG
FINAL: NG

Pronunciation

"NG" AS IN "BRI**NG**"
"NG" AS IN "BRI**NG**"

IPA and Tonal Class

IPA: /ŋ/
IPA: /ŋ/

CLASS: LOW

Trace and Learn

Example Font Variations

ง
ง
ง

� card card card card card card card card card card card card card

 card

 card

 card

ჳ ჳ ჳ ჳ ჳ ჳ ჳ ჳ ჳ ჳ ჳ ჳ ჳ ჳ

ჳ

ჳ

ჳ

จ

จอ

JAAW (MID TONE)

Transliteration

INITIAL: CH
FINAL: T

Pronunciation

SIMILAR TO THE "CH" IN "**CH**AIR"
SIMILAR TO THE "T" IN "OU**T**"

IPA and Tonal Class

IPA: /tɕ/
IPA: /t̚/

CLASS: MID

Trace and Learn

Example Font Variations

จ

จ

จ

ךךךךךךךךךך

ך

ק

ק

ק

ךךךךךךךךךךךךךך

ק

ק

ק

ק

ฉอ

CHAAW (HIGH TONE)

Transliteration

INITIAL: CH

FINAL: -

Pronunciation

SIMILAR TO THE "CH" IN "**CH**AIR"
BUT ASPIRATED (WITH A PUFF OF
AIR RELEASED AT THE END).

IPA and Tonal Class

IPA: /tɕʰ/

IPA: / - /

CLASS: HIGH

Trace and Learn

Example Font Variations

ชอ

CHAAW (LOW TONE)

Transliteration

INITIAL: CH

FINAL: T

Pronunciation

SIMILAR TO THE "CH" IN "CHAIR" BUT ASPIRATED
(WITH A PUFF OF AIR RELEASED AT THE END).

"T" AS IN "OUT"

IPA and Tonal Class

IPA: /tɕʰ/

IPA: /t̚/

CLASS: LOW

Trace and Learn

Example Font Variations

ซอ

SAAW (HIGH TONE)

Transliteration

INITIAL: S

FINAL: T

Pronunciation

"S" AS IN "**S**CHOOL"

"T" AS IN "OU**T**"

IPA and Tonal Class

IPA: /s/

IPA: /t̚/

CLASS: LOW

Trace and Learn

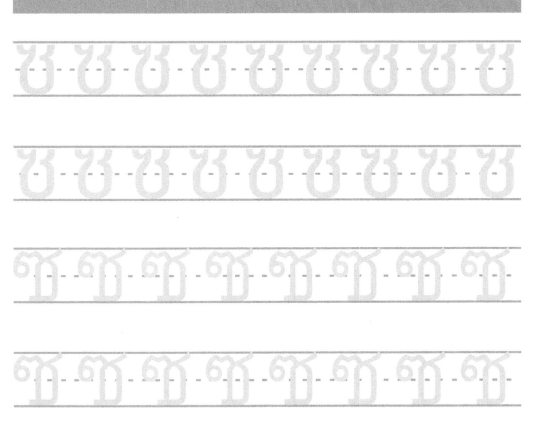

Example Font Variations

ฌ อ

CHAAW (LOW TONE)

Transliteration

INITIAL: CH

FINAL: -

Pronunciation

SIMILAR TO THE "CH" IN "CHAIR" BUT ASPIRATED (WITH A PUFF OF AIR RELEASED AT THE END).

IPA and Tonal Class

IPA: /tεʰ/

IPA: / - /

CLASS: LOW

Trace and Learn

Example Font Variations

ຓ ຓ ຓ ຓ ຓ ຓ ຓ ຓ

ຓ

ຓ

ຓ

ເຓ ເຓ ເຓ ເຓ ເຓ ເຓ ເຓ ເຓ ເຓ ເຓ

ເຓ

ເຓ

ເຓ

ເຓ

ញ្ញ

Yaaw (Low Tone)

Transliteration

INITIAL: Y
FINAL: N

Pronunciation

"Y" AS IN "**Y**ES"
"N" AS IN "FI**N**D"

IPA and Tonal Class

IPA: / j /
IPA: /n/

CLASS: LOW

Trace and Learn

Example Font Variations

ດໍ

DAAW (MID TONE)

Transliteration	Pronunciation	IPA and Tonal Class
INITIAL: D	"D" AS IN "DICE"	IPA: / d /
FINAL: T	"T" AS IN "TELL"	IPA: / t /

CLASS: MID

Trace and Learn

Example Font Variations

ຕໍ

DTAAW (MID TONE)

Transliteration	Pronunciation	IPA and Tonal Class
INITIAL: T	"T" AS IN "TELL"	IPA: / t /
FINAL: T	"T" AS IN "OUT"	IPA: / t̄ / CLASS: MID

Trace and Learn

Example Font Variations

ຖື

THAAW (HIGH TONE)

Transliteration

INITIAL: TH
FINAL: T

Pronunciation

"T" AS IN "**T**ALK"
"T" AS IN "OU**T**"

IPA and Tonal Class

IPA: /tʰ/
IPA: /t̄/

CLASS: HIGH

Trace and Learn

Example Font Variations

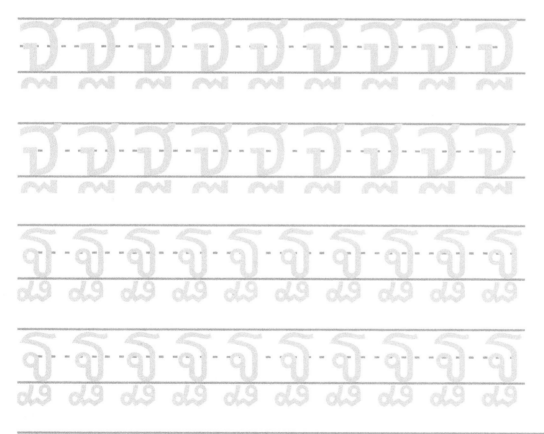

ฑอ

THAAW (LOW TONE)

Transliteration

INITIAL: Th
FINAL: T

Pronunciation

"T" AS IN "**T**ALK"
"T" AS IN "OU**T**"

IPA and Tonal Class

IPA: /tʰ/
IPA: /t̄/

CLASS: LOW

Trace and Learn

Example Font Variations

ฑ

ฑ

ฑ

ก ก ก ก ก ก ก ก ก ก ก ก

ก

ก

ก

ฤ ฤ ฤ ฤ ฤ ฤ ฤ ฤ ฤ ฤ

ฤ

ฤ

ฤ

ฒอ

THAAW (LOW TONE)

Transliteration

INITIAL: TH
FINAL: T

Pronunciation

"T" AS IN "TALK"
"T" AS IN "OUT"

IPA and Tonal Class

IPA: /tʰ/
IPA: /t̄/

CLASS: LOW

Trace and Learn

Example Font Variations

ณอ

Naaw (Low Tone)

Modern Print

Traditional Print

Transliteration	Pronunciation	IPA and Tonal Class
INITIAL: N	"N" AS IN "**N**O"	IPA: /n/
FINAL: N	"N" AS IN "**N**O"	IPA: /n/ CLASS: LOW

Trace and Learn

Example Font Variations

ณ ณ ณ ณ ณ ณ

ณ ณ ณ ณ ณ ณ

ณ ณ ณ ณ ณ ณ

ณ ณ ณ ณ ณ ณ

ณ ณ ณ ณ ณ ณ

ณ ณ ณ ณ ณ ณ ณ ณ

ณ

ณ

ณ

เณ เณ เณ เณ เณ เณ เณ เณ

เณ

เณ

เณ

เณ

ดอ

DAAW (MID TONE)

Modern Print

Traditional Print

Transliteration

INITIAL: D
FINAL: T

Pronunciation

"D" AS IN "**D**ICE"
"T" AS IN "OU**T**"

IPA and Tonal Class

IPA: / d /
IPA: / t̄ /

CLASS: MID

Trace and Learn

Example Font Variations

42

ଅ ଅ ଅ ଅ ଅ ଅ ଅ ଅ ଅ ଅ ଅ ଅ ଅ ଅ

ଅ

ଅ

ଅ

ଋ ଋ ଋ ଋ ଋ ଋ ଋ ଋ ଋ ଋ ଋ ଋ ଋ

ଋ

ଋ

ଋ

ଋ

ต

ตอ

DTAAW (MID TONE)

Transliteration

INITIAL: T

FINAL: T

Pronunciation

"T" AS IN "TELL"

"T" AS IN "OUT"

IPA and Tonal Class

IPA: / t /

IPA: / t̄ /

CLASS: MID

Trace and Learn

Example Font Variations

ถอ

THAAW (HIGH TONE)

Transliteration	**Pronunciation**	**IPA and Tonal Class**
INITIAL: TH	"T" AS IN "**T**ALK"	IPA: /tʰ/
FINAL: T	"T" AS IN "OU**T**"	IPA: /t̄/ CLASS: HIGH

Trace and Learn

Example Font Variations

ฑ

ทอ

THAAW (LOW TONE)

Transliteration

INITIAL: Th
FINAL: T

Pronunciation

"T" AS IN "**T**ALK"
"T" AS IN "OU**T**"

IPA and Tonal Class

IPA: /tʰ/
IPA: /t̄/

CLASS: LOW

Trace and Learn

Example Font Variations

n n n n n n n n n n

n

n

n

n n n n n n n n n n n

n

n

n

n

ธอ

THAAW (LOW TONE)

Transliteration	Pronunciation	IPA and Tonal Class
INITIAL: TH	"T" AS IN "**T**ALK"	IPA: /tʰ/
FINAL: T	"T" AS IN "OU**T**"	IPA: /t̄/ CLASS: LOW

Trace and Learn

Example Font Variations

น

นอ

NAAW (LOW TONE)

1 น 2

น
1

Transliteration

INITIAL: N
FINAL: N

Pronunciation

"N" AS IN "**N**O"
"N" AS IN "**N**O"

IPA and Tonal Class

IPA: /n/
IPA: /n/
CLASS: LOW

Trace and Learn

Example Font Variations

น

น

น

น

น

น

53

บอ

BAAW (MID TONE)

Modern Print

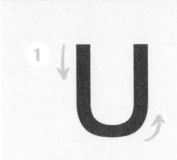

Traditional Print

Transliteration

INITIAL: B

FINAL: P

Pronunciation

"B" AS IN "**B**OAT"

"P" AS IN "A**P**T"

IPA and Tonal Clas

IPA: /b/

IPA: /p̄/

CLASS: MI

Trace and Learn

UUUUUUUUU

UUUUUUUUUU

บบบบบบบบบบ

บบบบบบบบบบ

บบบบบบบบบบบบบบ

Example Fon
Variations

ปอ

BPAAW (MID TONE)

Modern Print

Traditional Print

Transliteration

INITIAL: P

FINAL: P

Pronunciation

"P" AS IN "PUT"

"P" AS IN "APT"

IPA and Tonal Class

IPA: /p/

IPA: /p̄/

CLASS: MID

Trace and Learn

Example Font Variations

ปปปป

56

ผอ

PHAAW (HIGH TONE)

Transliteration

INITIAL: PH

FINAL: -

Pronunciation

"P" AS IN "PACK"

IPA and Tonal Clas

IPA: /pʰ/

IPA: / - /

CLASS: HIG

Trace and Learn

Example Fon
Variations

ฝอ

FAAW (HIGH TONE)

Modern Print

Traditional Print

Transliteration

INITIAL: F

FINAL: -

Pronunciation

"F" AS IN "FROM"

IPA and Tonal Class

IPA: / f /

IPA: / - /

CLASS: HIGH

Trace and Learn

Example Font Variations

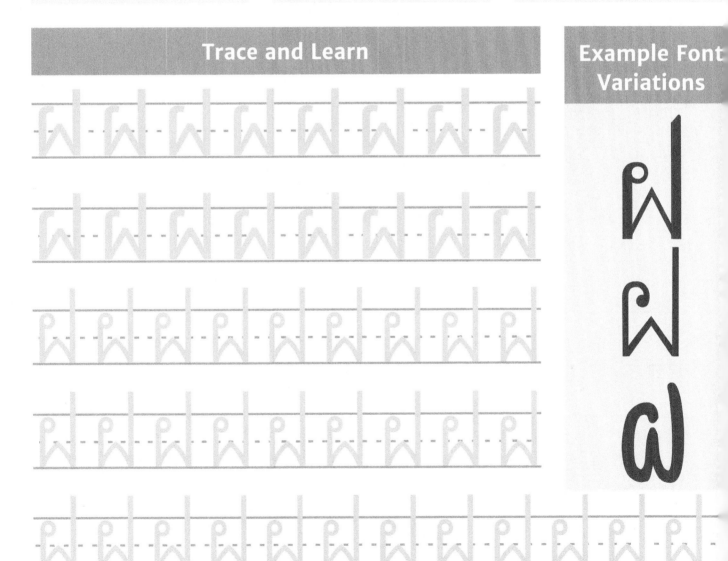

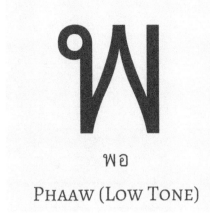

พอ

PHAAW (LOW TONE)

Transliteration

INITIAL: PH

FINAL: P

Pronunciation

"P" AS IN "PACK"

"P" AS IN "APT"

IPA and Tonal Class

IPA: /pʰ/

IPA: /p̄/

CLASS: LOW

Trace and Learn

Example Font Variations

62

WWWWWWWWWW

W

W

W

W W W W W W W W W W

W

W

W

W

ฟอ

FAAW (LOW TONE)

Modern Print

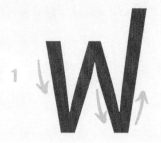

Traditional Print

Transliteration

INITIAL: F

FINAL: P

Pronunciation

"F" AS IN "**F**ROM"

"P" AS IN "A**P**T"

IPA and Tonal Class

IPA: / f /

IPA: / p̄ /

CLASS: LOW

Trace and Learn

Example Font Variations

ภอ

PHAAW (LOW TONE)

Transliteration

INITIAL: PH

FINAL: P

Pronunciation

"P" AS IN "PACK"

"P" AS IN "APT"

IPA and Tonal Class

IPA: /pʰ/

IPA: /p̄/

CLASS: LOW

Trace and Learn

Example Font Variations

ม

มอ

MAAW (LOW TONE)

Modern Print

Traditional Print

Transliteration

INITIAL: M
FINAL: M

Pronunciation

"M" AS IN "MORE"
"M" AS IN "MORE"

IPA and Tonal Class

IPA: /m/
IPA: /m/
CLASS: LOW

Trace and Learn

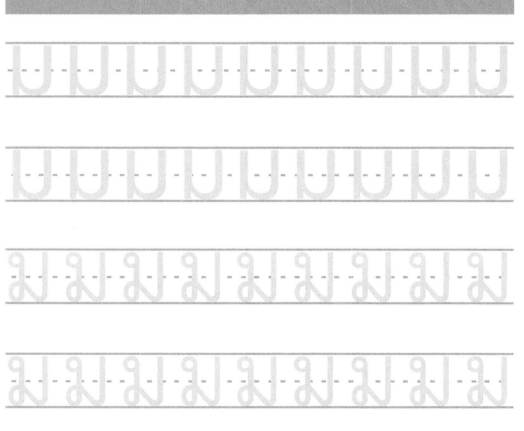

Example Font Variations

ຍ

ຍໍ

YAAW (LOW TONE)

Transliteration

INITIAL: Y
FINAL: - OR N

Pronunciation

"Y" AS IN "YOU"
"N" AS IN "NO"

IPA and Tonal Class

IPA: / j /
IPA: / n /

CLASS: LOW

Trace and Learn

Example Font Variations

70

รอ

RAAW (MID TONE)

Transliteration

INITIAL: R

FINAL: N

Pronunciation

"R" AS IN "RED"

"N" AS IN "NO"

IPA and Tonal Class

IPA: / r /

IPA: / n /

CLASS: LOW

Trace and Learn

Example Font Variations

SSSSSSSSSS

SSSSSSSSSS

รรรรรรรรรร

รรรรรรรรรร

รรรรรรรรรรรรรรรร

73

ลอ

LAAW (LOW TONE)

Transliteration

INITIAL: L

FINAL: N

Pronunciation

"L" AS IN "LOVE"

"N" AS IN "NO"

IPA and Tonal Class

IPA: / l /

IPA: / n /

CLASS: LOW

Trace and Learn

Example Font Variations

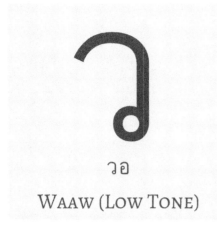

วอ

WAAW (LOW TONE)

Transliteration

INITIAL: W

FINAL: -

Pronunciation

"W" AS IN "WHAT

IPA and Tonal Class

IPA: / w /

IPA: / - /

CLASS: LOW

Trace and Learn

Example Font Variations

ศอ

SAAW (HIGH TONE)

Modern Print

Traditional Print

Transliteration

INITIAL: S
FINAL: T

Pronunciation

"S" AS IN "**S**OME"
"T" AS IN "OU**T**"

IPA and Tonal Class

IPA: / s /
IPA: / t̄ /

CLASS: HIGH

Trace and Learn

Example Font Variations

ษอ

SAAW (HIGH TONE)

Transliteration

INITIAL: S
FINAL: T

Pronunciation

"S" AS IN "**S**OME"
"T" AS IN "OU**T**"

IPA and Tonal Class

IPA: / s /
IPA: / t̄ /
CLASS: HIGH

Trace and Learn

Example Font Variations

สอ

SAAW (HIGH TONE)

Modern Print

Traditional Print

Transliteration

INITIAL: S
FINAL: T

Pronunciation

"S" AS IN "SOME"
"T" AS IN "OUT"

IPA and Tonal Class

IPA: / s /
IPA: / t̄ /

CLASS: HIGH

Trace and Learn

Example Font Variations

ห

หอ

HAAW (HIGH TONE)

Transliteration

INITIAL: H

FINAL: -

Pronunciation

"H" AS IN "HOW"

IPA and Tonal Class

IPA: / h /

IPA: / - /

CLASS: HIGH

Trace and Learn

Example Font Variations

ห

ห

ห

ฬอ

LAAW (LOW TONE)

Transliteration

INITIAL: L
FINAL: N

Pronunciation

"L" AS IN "LOVE"
"N" AS IN "NO"

IPA and Tonal Class

IPA: / l /
IPA: / n /

CLASS: LOW

Trace and Learn

Example Font Variations

ฬ

ฬ

ฬ

ฟ ฟ ฟ ฟ ฟ ฟ ฟ ฟ ฟ

ฟ

ฟ

ฟ

ฟ ฟ ฟ ฟ ฟ ฟ ฟ ฟ ฟ

ฟ

ฟ

ฟ

ฟ

ອ ອ

AAAW (MID TONE)

Modern Print

Traditional Print

Transliteration

INITIAL: -

FINAL: -

Pronunciation

-

IPA and Tonal Class

IPA: / ʔ /

IPA: / - /

CLASS: MID

Trace and Learn

Example Font Variations

ຫໍ

HAAW (LOW TONE)

Modern Print

1 2

Traditional Print

1

Transliteration

INITIAL: H
FINAL: -

Pronunciation

"H" AS IN "HOW"

IPA and Tonal Class

IPA: /h/
IPA: /-/

CLASS: LOW

Trace and Learn

Example Font Variations

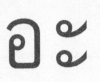				
A	A	A	I	I
IPA: /a/	IPA: /a/	IPA: /a:/	IPA: /i/	IPA: /i:/

Ue	Ue	Ue	U	U
IPA: /ɯ/	IPA: /ɯ:/	IPA: /ɯ:/	IPA: /u/	IPA: /u:/

E	E	E	Ae	Ae
IPA: /e/	IPA: /e/	IPA: /e:/	IPA: /ɛ/	IPA: /ɛ/

Ae	O	O	O	O
IPA: /ɛ:/	IPA: /o/	IPA: /o:/	IPA: /ɔ/	IPA: /ɔ/
		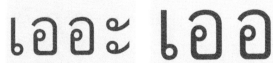		
O	O	Oe	Oe	Ae
IPA: /ɔ:/	IPA: /ɔ:/	IPA: /ɤʔ/	IPA: /ɤ:/	IPA: /ɤ:/

เอียะ	เอีย	เอียะ	เอือ	อัวะ
IA	IA	UEA	UEA	UA
IPA: /iaʔ/	IPA: /ia/	IPA: /ɯaʔ/	IPA: /ɯa/	IPA: /uaʔ/

อัว	อว	อิว	เอ็อ	เอว
UA	UA	IO	EO	EO
IPA: /ua/	IPA: /ua/	IPA: /iu/ OR /iw/	IPA: /eu/ OR /ew/	IPA: /e:u/ OR /e:w/

แอว	เอา	อาว	เอียว	อัย
AEO	AO	AO	IAO	AI
IPA: /ɛ:u/ OR /ɛ:w/	IPA: /au/ OR /aw/	IPA: /a:u/	IPA: /iau/ OR /iaw/	IPA: /ɔi/ OR /ɔj/

ใอ	ไอ	ไอย	อาย	อ็อย
AI	AI	AI	AI	OI
IPA: /ai/ OR /aj/	IPA: /ai/ OR /aj/	IPA: /ai/ OR /aj/	IPA: /a:i/ OR /a:j/	IPA: /ɔi/ OR /ɔj/

ออย	โอย	อุย	เอย	อวย
OI	OI	UI	OEI	UAI
IPA: /ɔ:i/ OR /ɔ:j/	IPA: /o:i/ OR /o:j/	IPA: /ui/ OR /uj/	IPA: /ɤ:j/	IPA: /uaj/

เอือย	อำ	ฤ RUE	ฦ RUE	ฦ LUE
UEAI	AM	IPA: /rɯ/ OR /ri/	IPA: /rɯ:/	IPA: /lɯ/
IPA: /ɯai/ OR /ɯaj/	IPA: /am/	ฦ LUE	อ็ำ M	อ์ SILENT
		IPA: /lɯ:/	IPA: /~/	

In the following pages you'll find ample space to train your ability to handwrite these vowels, diphthongs.

Feel free to photocopy the pages as needed.

96

97

เอะ เอะ เอะ เอะ เอะ เอ

เอะ เอะ เอะ เอะ เอะ เอ

เอะ เอะ เอะ เอะ เอะ เอ

เอะ เอะ เอะ เอะ เอะ เอ

เอ เอ เอ เอ เอ เอ เอ เอ

เอ เอ เอ เอ เอ เอ เอ

เอ เอ เอ เอ เอ เอ เอ

เอ เอ เอ เอ เอ เอ เอ

เอ เอ เอ เอ เอ เอ เอ เอ

เอ เอ เอ เอ เอ เอ เอ เอ

เอ เอ เอ เอ เอ เอ เอ เอ

เอ เอ เอ เอ เอ เอ เอ เอ

แอะ แอะ แอะ แอะ แอะ

แอะ แอะ แอะ แอะ แอะ

แอะ แอะ แอะ แอะ แอะ

แอะ แอะ แอะ แอะ แอะ

แด แด แด แด แด แด แด

แด แด แด แด แด แด แด

แว แว แว แว แว แว

แว แว แว แว แว แว

แด แด แด แด แด แด

แด แด แด แด แด แด

แว แว แว แว แว

แว แว แว แว แว

เอะ เอะ เอะ เอะ เอะ

เอะ เอะ เอะ เอะ เอะ

โอะ โอะ โอะ โอะ โอะ

โอะ โอะ โอะ โอะ โอะ

เอ เอ เอ เอ เอ เอ เอ เอ

เอ เอ เอ เอ เอ เอ เอ เอ

โอ โอ โอ โอ โอ โอ โอ โอ

โอ โอ โอ โอ โอ โอ โอ โอ

เอาะ เอาะ เอาะ เอาะ

เอาะ เอาะ เอาะ เอาะ

เอาะ เอาะ เอาะ เอาะ

เอาะ เอาะ เอาะ เอาะ

ออ ออ ออ ออ ออ ออ ออ

ออ ออ ออ ออ ออ ออ ออ

ออ ออ ออ ออ ออ ออ

ออ ออ ออ ออ ออ ออ

ดี ดี ดี ดี ดี ดี ดี ดี ดี ดี ดี
ดี ดี ดี ดี ดี ดี ดี ดี ดี ดี ดี

ดู ดู ดู ดู ดู ดู ดู ดู ดู ดู ดู
ดู ดู ดู ดู ดู ดู ดู ดู ดู ดู ดู

เดอะ เดอะ เดอะ เดอะ

เดอะ เดอะ เดอะ เดอะ

เออะ เออะ เออะ เออะ

เออะ เออะ เออะ เออะ

เอียะ เอียะ เอียะ เอียะ

เอียะ เอียะ เอียะ เอียะ

เอียะ เอียะ เอียะ เอียะ

เอียะ เอียะ เอียะ เอียะ

เอีย เอีย เอีย เอีย เอีย เอีย

เอีย เอีย เอีย เอีย เอีย เอีย

เอีย เอีย เอีย เอีย เอีย

เอีย เอีย เอีย เอีย เอีย

เอียะ เอียะ เอียะ เอียะ

เอียะ เอียะ เอียะ เอียะ

เอียะ เอียะ เอียะ เอียะ

เอียะ เอียะ เอียะ เอียะ

เอือ เอือ เอือ เอือ เอือ

เอือ เอือ เอือ เอือ เอือ

เออ เออ เออ เออ เออ

เออ เออ เออ เออ เออ

110

เออ เออ เออ เออ เออ เออ

เออ เออ เออ เออ เออ เออ

เออ เออ เออ เออ เออ

เออ เออ เออ เออ เออ

เอว เอว เอว เอว เอว

เอว เอว เอว เอว เอว

เอ เอ เอ เอ เอ

เอ เอ เอ เอ เอ

แอว แอว แอว แอว แอว

แอว แอว แอว แอว แอว

แอว แอว แอว แอว

แอว แอว แอว แอว

เอา เอา เอา เอา เอา เอา

เอา เอา เอา เอา เอา

เอา เอา เอา เอา เอา

เอา เอา เอา เอา เอา

อาว อาว อาว อาว อาว

อาว อาว อาว อาว อาว

อาว อาว อาว อาว อาว

อาว อาว อาว อาว อาว

เอียว เอียว เอียว เอียว

เอียว เอียว เอียว เอียว

เอียว เอียว เอียว เอียว

เอียว เอียว เอียว เอียว

อาย - อาย - อาย - อาย - อาย

อาย - อาย - อาย - อาย - อาย

อาย - อาย - อาย - อาย - อาย

อาย - อาย - อาย - อาย - อาย

ออย - ออย - ออย - ออย - ออย

ออย - ออย - ออย - ออย - ออย

ออย - ออย - ออย - ออย

ออย - ออย - ออย - ออย

ออย - ออย - ออย - ออย - ออย

ออย - ออย - ออย - ออย - ออย

ออย - ออย - ออย - ออย

ออย - ออย - ออย - ออย

โอย โอย โอย โอย โอย

โอย โอย โอย โอย โอย

โอย โอย โอย โอย โอย

โอย โอย โอย โอย โอย

อวย อวย อวย อวย อวย

อวย อวย อวย อวย อวย

อวย อวย อวย อวย

อวย อวย อวย อวย

เออย เออย เออย เออย

เออย เออย เออย เออย

เออย เออย เออย เออย

เออย เออย เออย เออย

123

Made in the USA
Las Vegas, NV
19 October 2024

10077004R00070